JANET DRAUGHN

10 Email Hacks to Optimize Your Productivity

How to Reduce Clutter, Relieve Stress, and Focus on What's Important

For Kaitlin

Contents

1

Introduction

Email has revolutionized the way we communicate, offering unparalleled convenience and speed. It has become an indispensable tool in both our personal and professional lives, enabling us to connect with others across the globe in an instant. From coordinating business deals to staying in touch with loved ones, our inboxes serve as digital hubs for communication. However, along with its many benefits, email has also brought about its own set of challenges.

In today's fast-paced world, every minute counts and multitasking has become the norm. The volume of emails we receive can quickly become overwhelming, leading to stress and a sense of being constantly behind. Many of us find ourselves drowning in a sea of unread messages. Do you struggle to keep your inbox under control? You are not alone.

As the author of this book, I understand firsthand the struggles and frustrations that accompany the relentless onslaught of emails. I have experienced the dread of an overflowing inbox and the anxiety of constantly feeling behind. But through trial and error, I have discovered strategies that have transformed my relationship with email—from a source of chaos to a tool for efficiency and clarity.

This book is designed to be your life raft, offering you ten essential hacks to help you tame the email beast, reduce your stress, and reclaim your productivity. Whether you are a business professional inundated with work emails or a busy parent trying to stay on top of personal correspondence, these hacks will empower you to take control of your inbox and focus on what truly matters.

In the pages that follow, I will share with you a collection of ten powerful hacks designed to revolutionize the way you approach email. Each hack is practical, actionable, and easy to implement, ensuring that you can start seeing results immediately. From turning off notifications to using labels and filters effectively, these hacks will transform the way you approach email, making it a tool that enhances your efficiency rather than hinders it.

By the end of this book, you will have the tools and strategies you need to revolutionize your email habits, allowing you to spend less time in your inbox and more time on the things that bring you joy and fulfillment. So, are you ready to take the first step towards a more organized, stress-free email experience? Let's dive in!

2

Email Habits - The Good and the Bad

Email has become such an integral part of our daily lives that the way we interact with it has developed into habits, some of which can either support our productivity or create unnecessary stress. In this chapter, we will explore these habits, categorizing them into the good and the bad, and discuss strategies to cultivate positive habits while breaking free from the negative ones.

Bad Habits

Hoarding: One of the most common bad habits when it comes to email is hoarding. This involves keeping a large number of emails in your inbox, often unread or unsorted. Hoarding emails can lead to a cluttered inbox, making it difficult to find important messages when you need them.

Ignoring: Ignoring emails is another bad habit that can lead to missed opportunities and strained relationships. Whether it is failing to respond to important emails or simply letting messages pile up without taking any action, ignoring emails can quickly spiral out of control.

Poor filing: Effective email management relies on a well-organized filing system. However, many people fall into the bad habit of filing emails haphazardly or failing to file them at all. This can make it challenging to locate specific emails when you need them, leading to wasted time and frustration.

Good Habits

Be Concise and Get to the Point: It is important to realize that no one has the time to read an email full of useless information. You must learn to respect your recipients' time by getting to the point quickly. Start your emails off with the most vital information and try to avoid the unnecessary fluff. Ask yourself if you would want this much detail if you were the receiver.

Use Descriptive Subject Lines: Clear subject lines help recipients understand the purpose of your email. By starting your emails with a clear subject line, your reader can more easily recognize what the body of the email will be about. Try to avoid using vague or generic subjects like "Hi" or "Question" that do not tell the reader anything about what is to come.

Watch Your Tone and Language: Regardless of who the emails are going to, you should always be professional and courteous. Using all caps should be avoided, as many people interpret this as shouting and can be perceived as bad manners. Be aware of overly formal or informal language when sending emails. Always take into consideration the audience and use the right tone.

Be responsive: Finally, one of the best habits you can cultivate is being responsive to emails. This does not mean you have to reply immediately to every message, but aim to respond in a timely manner, especially to important or time-sensitive emails.

By cultivating these good habits and breaking free from the bad ones, you can transform your email experience from a source of stress and overwhelm to a tool for productivity and efficiency. You never want to lose your reader before they have had time to get the meaning of your message.

3

Hack #1 - Turn off notifications when focusing on a task

The ability to focus on a single task without distractions has become a rare skill. From emails to social media updates, our devices are constantly vying for our attention, pulling us away from the task at hand. In this chapter, we will explore the impact of notifications on our productivity and discuss a simple yet powerful hack to help you stay focused and minimize distractions.

Focus on the Task at Hand and Ignore All Other Things for Short Intervals

One of the key principles of productivity is the ability to focus deeply on the task at hand. However, constant notifications can disrupt this focus, pulling your attention away and making it difficult to re-engage with your work. To combat this, try setting short intervals of focused work time, during which you ignore all notifications and distractions. Close unnecessary tabs on your browser, put your phone on silent, and eliminate any other potential distractions. Even just 25 minutes of focused work, followed by a short break, can lead to significant improvements in productivity. This will allow you to dive deep into your work without interruptions, increasing your productivity and the quality of your output.

Notifications Are Interruptions That Make It Hard to Re-Engage Your Mind on the Task at Hand

Research has shown that notifications are more than just a minor annoyance—they can have a significant impact on your ability to focus and perform tasks effectively. It is estimated that 40% of your productivity is lost when you multi-task (Weinschenk, 2012). Each time you are interrupted by a notification, it takes time for your brain to re-orient itself back to the task at hand, leading to a phenomenon known as "task-switching cost." This cost can be substantial, resulting in decreased productivity and an increased likelihood of errors.

By turning off notifications during focused work time, you can minimize these interruptions and improve your ability to stay on task. This simple hack can have a profound impact on your productivity, allowing you to accomplish more in less time and with greater focus. You can retrain your brain to ignore distractions and improve your focus.

4

Hack #2 - Reduce the Volume of Unnecessary Emails

Are your email inboxes are flooded with an overwhelming number of messages, many of which serve no real purpose? From marketing emails to promotional offers, it seems like everyone wants a piece of our attention. In this chapter, we will delve into the strategies for minimizing the influx of unnecessary emails and reclaiming control over our inboxes.

Unsubscribe to Junk Email - Check Regularly

One of the most effective ways to reduce the volume of unnecessary emails is to unsubscribe from mailing lists and newsletters that no longer serve a purpose. Take a proactive approach to managing your subscriptions by regularly reviewing the emails you receive and unsubscribing from any that are no longer relevant or useful. Most emails include an unsubscribe link at the bottom, making it easy to opt out with just a few clicks. By decluttering your inbox in this way, you can free up valuable mental space and ensure that only the most important messages make it to your attention.

Be Cautious When Giving Out Your Email Address

Another key strategy for reducing unnecessary emails is to be selective about who you share your email address with. Avoid giving out your email indiscriminately, especially on websites or forms that may sell or distribute your information to third parties. Instead, consider creating a separate email address specifically for promotional purposes, allowing you to keep your primary inbox free from unwanted clutter.

Even if It Only Takes 10 Seconds to Deal with an Unnecessary Email, 10 Emails per Day at 10 Seconds Each for 5 Days for 52 Weeks Is a Loss of Over 7 Hours a Year

It is easy to underestimate the cumulative impact of dealing with unnecessary emails, but even a few seconds spent on each message can quickly add up over time. Consider this: if you spend just 10 seconds dealing with each unnecessary email and receive ten such emails per day, that's one hundred seconds—or over 1.5 minutes—of wasted time each day. Multiply that by five days a week and 52 weeks a year, and you are looking at a loss of over 7 hours annually. That's 7 hours that could be spent on more productive or enjoyable pursuits.

By taking proactive steps to unsubscribe from junk email, being cautious about sharing your email address, and recognizing the hidden costs of dealing with unnecessary emails, you can significantly reduce the volume of clutter in your inbox and reclaim valuable time and mental bandwidth. So, the next time you find yourself inundated with promotional offers and irrelevant messages, remember these simple yet powerful strategies for regaining control over your email and optimizing your productivity.

5

Hack #3 - Use a Signature Line

Within the context of email etiquette and productivity, the unassuming signature line often goes unnoticed. However, it serves a more significant purpose than a mere farewell in your emails. A well-crafted signature line can elevate professionalism, streamline communication, and make a lasting impact on your recipients. In the following section, we will delve into the advantages of utilizing a signature line and offer guidance on creating an impactful one.

Creates a Strong First Impression

Your email signature is often the first thing recipients see when they open your message, making it a valuable opportunity to make a positive impact. A well-crafted signature can convey professionalism, attention to detail, and a sense of trustworthiness. Include your name, job title, and company name to establish your identity and credibility right from the start.

Verifies Identity

In an age where phishing scams and identity theft are rampant, a signature line can serve as a form of verification. By including your full name and contact information in your signature, you provide recipients with a way to verify your identity and ensure that the email is legitimate. This can help build trust and reduce the likelihood of your emails being mistaken for spam.

Provides Important Contact Information

A signature line is also a convenient way to provide recipients with your contact information, such as your phone number, email address, and physical address. This makes it easy for recipients to contact you without having to search for your contact details elsewhere. Additionally, including links to your social media profiles or website can further enhance your professional image and provide recipients with additional ways to connect with you. On a professional note, you can provide an assistant's contact information below your signature to help with future communications.

Improves Efficiency Without Having to Type the Same Information Each Time

Another key benefit of using a signature line is the time and effort it saves. Instead of typing out your contact information and sign-off every time you send an email, you can simply include it in your signature and have it automatically appended to your messages. This not only saves time but also ensures consistency in your communications, as all your emails will have the same professional sign-off.

A signature line is a simple yet powerful tool that can enhance your professionalism, improve efficiency, and have a positive impact on your recipients. By including your information in your signature, you can establish your identity, verify your legitimacy, and provide recipients with a convenient way to contact you. So, the next time you compose an email, do not overlook the power of a well-crafted signature line—it could be the key to making a lasting impression.

6

Hack #4 - Deal with Emails Only Once

One of the biggest productivity killers is indecision in this information day and age. When you read an email but do not act immediately, you create re-work for yourself. You waste time by having to re-read the email and decide what to do with it a second or even third time. In this chapter, we will explore the importance of dealing with emails only once and provide strategies for managing them efficiently.

If You Can Take Care of It in Two Minutes or Less, Do It Now

One of the simplest and most effective strategies for dealing with emails is the two-minute rule. If you receive an email that requires a quick response or action that can be completed in two minutes or less, do it immediately. This prevents the email from lingering in your inbox and ensures that simple tasks are taken care of promptly. By following this rule, you can significantly reduce the number of emails that require further action and free up valuable time for more important tasks.

File, Move into an Action Folder, or Delete

For emails that require more than two minutes of your time, it is important to take decisive action. After reading the email, immediately file it into a relevant folder, move it into an action folder for tasks that require follow-up, or delete it if it is no longer needed. This prevents emails from cluttering your inbox and ensures that you have a clear action plan for each message. By dealing with emails only once and taking action, you can streamline your email workflow and avoid the inefficiencies of re-work.

Dealing with emails only once is a key strategy for improving productivity and efficiency in your email management. By following the two-minute rule for quick tasks and acting on all other emails, you can reduce the amount of re-work you create for yourself and ensure that your inbox remains organized and manageable. So, the next time you open your inbox, remember the importance of dealing with emails promptly and decisively—it is the key to staying on top of your workload and minimizing wasted time.

7

Hack #5 - Dedicate Email Only Time

Our email inboxes can easily become a source of distraction and overwhelm. With emails pouring in constantly, it can be challenging to stay focused and productive. One effective strategy for managing your inbox and maintaining control over your day is to dedicate specific time each day to deal with emails. In this chapter, we will explore the benefits of dedicating email-only time and provide tips for maximizing its effectiveness.

Check Emails Early Each Day for an Allotted Amount of Time

One primary way to manage your inbox is to check your emails early each day for a specific, allotted amount of time. This allows you to start your day with a clear understanding of what needs to be addressed and prioritize your tasks accordingly. By setting aside dedicated time for emails, you can avoid the temptation to constantly check your inbox throughout the day, which can be a major source of distraction.

Recheck Email Inbox 4-5 Throughout the Day and Let It Sit the Rest of the Day

In addition to checking your emails early in the day, it can be helpful to schedule additional times throughout the day to recheck your inbox. Aim for 4-5 times per day, spaced out at regular intervals. This allows you to stay on top of new emails without letting them consume your entire day. Outside of these designated times, resist the urge to constantly check your inbox and instead focus on other tasks that require your attention.

Benefits of a Zero Inbox

One of the key benefits of dedicating email-only time is the ability to achieve a "zero inbox" at the end of each session. A zero inbox means that you have processed and dealt with all the emails in your inbox, leaving it empty or nearly empty. Zero inbox can be described as a productivity strategy to methodically manage the chaos (Martins, 2024). This can provide a sense of accomplishment and clarity, knowing that you have addressed all outstanding emails and have a clear slate for the next day. Additionally, a zero inbox can help reduce the mental burden of a cluttered inbox and make it easier to stay organized and focused.

Dedicating specific time each day to manage your inbox can be a highly effective strategy for improving productivity and reducing stress. By checking your emails early each day, rechecking them at regular intervals, and aiming for a zero inbox at the end of each session, you can stay on top of your emails and maintain control over your day. So, the next time you open your inbox, consider setting aside dedicated email-only time—it could be the key to a more organized and productive day.

Hack #6 - Create Templates

Most of the daily emails we send contain the same or similar information, such as responses to frequently asked questions or standard updates. Creating email templates can be a game-changer, allowing you to quickly compose emails that are both accurate and consistent. In this chapter, we will explore the benefits of using templates and provide tips for creating effective ones.

Benefits Include Reducing Errors, Optimizing Your Workflow, and Improves Response Time

One of the primary benefits of using email templates is that they can help reduce errors. By pre-writing your responses and saving them as templates, you can ensure not to overlook or omit essential information. This can be particularly useful for complex or technical information that must be communicated accurately.

Another benefit of using templates is that they can optimize your workflow. Instead of spending time composing the same email repeatedly, you can simply select a template and customize it as needed.

This can save you valuable time and allow you to focus on more important tasks.

Using templates can improve your response time. By having pre-written responses ready to go, you can reply to emails more quickly, which can be especially useful for time-sensitive inquiries or requests. If you analyze the responses, you typically send, you will see a lot of commonalities. This is exactly where template can become most useful. They can help you stay on top of your inbox and ensure that important messages are addressed promptly.

Creating email templates can be a valuable tool for improving efficiency and productivity in your email communication. By reducing errors, optimizing your workflow, and improving your response time, templates can help you manage your inbox more effectively and free up time for other tasks. So, the next time you find yourself composing the same email for the umpteenth time, consider creating a template—it could be the key to streamlining your email communication and improving your overall productivity.

9

Hack #7 - Use Out of Office Notification

When you are going to be away from work, use an out-of-office notification to alert people that you may not be able to respond to their email right away. It is important to keep your contacts informed when you are unavailable. Whether you are on vacation, attending a conference, or simply out of the office for the day, using an out-of-office (OOO) notification can help manage expectations and prevent frustration. In this chapter, we will explore the purpose of an out-of-office notification and provide tips for crafting an effective one.

Purpose - Alerts People That You Will Not Be Able to Respond

The primary purpose of an out-of-office notification is to alert people that you will not be able to respond to their emails immediately. This can help manage expectations and prevent misunderstandings. By setting up an out-of-office notification, you can let your contacts know that you are away from your desk and may not be able to reply to their emails until you return. You can even add a return date to let people know when they may expect you to return.

What to Include - When They Can Expect You Back and Whom to Contact in Case of an Emergency

When setting up an out-of-office notification, it is important to include key information such as when you expect to be back and whom to contact in case of an emergency. This helps provide clarity to your contacts and ensures that urgent matters are addressed in your absence. Be sure to include the date of your return and provide the name and contact information of a colleague or manager who can assist in your absence. Using this hack can keep people from sending you multiple emails during the time you are expected to be away.

Using an out-of-office notification can be a valuable tool for managing expectations and preventing frustration in your email communication. By alerting people that you are away from your desk and providing key information about your return date and whom to contact in case of an emergency, you can help ensure that your absence is managed smoothly. So, the next time you are away from work, consider setting up an out-of-office notification—it is a simple yet effective way to keep your contacts informed and manage your email communication effectively.

Hack #8 - Use Keyboard Shortcuts

Keyboard shortcuts are a powerful tool for improving efficiency and productivity in your email communication. By using keyboard shortcuts, you can reduce the number of keystrokes needed to accomplish a task, saving you time and effort. In this chapter, we will explore the benefits of using keyboard shortcuts and provide examples of common shortcuts for popular email programs like Gmail and Outlook.

5 Common Gmail Shortcuts (Duò, 2022)

1. Compose a new email: Press c to start composing a new email.
2. Send an email: Press Ctrl + Enter to send an email you have composed.
3. Archive an email: Press e to archive the selected email.
4. Move to the next email: Press j to move to the next email in your inbox.
5. Move to the previous email: Press k to move to the previous email in your inbox.

5 Common Outlook Shortcuts (Keyboard Shortcuts for Outlook, n.d.)

1. Compose a new email: Press Ctrl + N to start composing a new email.
2. Send an email: Press Ctrl + Enter to send an email you have composed.
3. Reply to an email: Press Ctrl + R to reply to the sender of the selected email.
4. Reply all to an email: Press Ctrl + Shift + R to reply to all recipients of the selected email.
5. Forward an email: Press Ctrl + F to forward the selected email.

Using keyboard shortcuts can be a valuable tool for improving efficiency and productivity in your email communication. By familiarizing yourself with common shortcuts for your email program, you can reduce the number of keystrokes needed to accomplish tasks and save time and effort. So, the next time you are composing an email or managing your inbox, consider using keyboard shortcuts—it is a simple yet effective way to streamline your workflow and produce more in less time.

11

Hack #9 - Use Labels and Filters

Staying organized is key to maintaining a clutter-free inbox and staying on top of important messages. One powerful tool for achieving this is the use of labels and filters. Available in most email clients, labels and filters can help you control spam, automate tasks, and sort through emails as they are received. In this chapter, we will explore how to use labels and filters effectively to streamline your email workflow.

Labels

Labels are a way to categorize and organize your emails. They allow you to visually identify emails at a glance and group related messages together. For example, you can create labels for different projects, clients, or categories and apply them to relevant emails. This makes it easy to find specific emails later and ensures that important messages do not get lost.

To create a label, simply open an email, click on the "Labels" button, and select "Create new." Give your label a name and choose a color to

23

help differentiate it from other labels. You can then apply this label to other emails by selecting them and choosing the label from the "Labels" menu.

Filters

Filters are a way to automate actions on incoming emails based on certain criteria. For example, you can set up a filter to automatically label and archive emails from a specific sender or with certain keywords. This can help you manage your inbox more efficiently and reduce the time spent manually sorting through emails.

To create a filter, check your email client for the filter option. Once you have found the option, create a new filter by entering the criteria for the filter. Examples of filters are the sender's email address or keywords in the subject line. You can then choose what action to take on emails that match your criteria, such as applying a label, archiving the email, or marking it as read. You can even move these emails to a folder or another email account as a way to manage information.

Labels and filters can be a powerful way to streamline your email workflow and stay organized. By categorizing emails with labels and automating actions with filters, you can ensure that important messages are easily accessible and that your inbox remains clutter-free. So, the next time you are faced with a mountain of emails, consider using labels and filters to help manage the load—it's a simple yet effective way to take control of your inbox.

Hack #10 - Use Emails to Create Tasks

Managing your tasks effectively is key to staying organized and on top of your workload. One powerful tool for task management is using emails to create tasks. This allows you to start a to-do list directly from your inbox, helping you track and prioritize your assignments. Various email programs offer features that allow you to create tasks directly from received emails, making it easy to turn emails into actionable items. In this chapter, we will explore what email tasks are and the benefits of using them in your workflow.

What Are Email Tasks

Email tasks are simply tasks that you create from emails you receive. They can be small or large assignments, personal or professional, that require action on your part. By turning emails into tasks, you can create a to-do list that helps you stay organized and focused on your priorities.

To create an email task, simply open the email you want to turn into a task and look for the option to create a task. This option is typically found in the toolbar or menu of your email client and may be labeled differently depending on the program you are using. Clicking on this option will create a task linked to the email, allowing you to reference the original message when you are ready to complete the task.

Benefits

There are several benefits to using emails to create tasks in your workflow:

1. Creates an Electronic To-Do List That You Can Access from Multiple Devices: By creating tasks from your emails, you create an electronic to-do list that you can access from multiple devices. This allows you to stay organized and keep track of your tasks no matter where you are.
2. Helps You Stay Organized: Email tasks help you stay organized by providing a central location for all your assignments. Instead of letting emails pile up in your inbox, you can convert them into tasks and prioritize them based on their importance and urgency.
3. Creates Reminders: Email tasks can also serve as reminders for upcoming deadlines or important events. Many email programs allow you to set due dates and reminders for tasks, ensuring that you stay on track and do not forget important tasks.

Using emails to create tasks can be a powerful tool for improving productivity and staying organized. By turning emails into actionable items, you can create a to-do list that helps you track and prioritize your assignments. So, the next time you receive an email that requires action, consider turning it into a task—it is a simple yet effective way to stay on top of your workload and achieve your goals.

13

Conclusion

Congratulations! You have reached the end of "10 Email Hacks to Optimize Your Productivity." Throughout this book, we have explored ten powerful hacks that can help you tame the email beast, reduce your stress, and increase your productivity. From managing your inbox more effectively to automating repetitive tasks, these hacks are designed to help you get the most out of your email communication.

As you reflect on the strategies and tips presented in this book, I encourage you to take action now and implement them into your daily routine. Start by identifying which hacks resonate most with you and begin incorporating them into your email workflow. Whether it is setting aside dedicated time for email management or creating templates for common responses, each hack has the potential to make a significant impact on your productivity and stress levels.

Remember, the goal of this book is not just to provide you with information, but to inspire you to take control of your email and transform it into a tool that enhances your productivity and reduces your stress. By adopting these hacks and making them a part of your daily routine, you can reclaim your inbox and focus on what truly matters.

I would love to hear your feedback on this book. If you found it helpful, please consider leaving a review on Amazon. Your review will not only help others discover the book but will also provide valuable feedback for future editions. Thank you for reading, and here is to a more productive and stress-free email experience!

14

Resources

Duò, M. (2022, December 22). *48 Handy Gmail keyboard shortcuts to supercharge your productivity. Kinsta®. https://kinsta.com/blog/gmail-keyboard-shortcuts/*

Keyboard shortcuts for Outlook. (n.d.). Support.microsoft.com. https://support.microsoft.com/en-us/office/keyboard-shortcuts-for-outlook-3cdeb221-7ae5-4c1d-8c1d-9e63216c1efd

Martins, J. (2024, January 2). *Inbox zero isn't what you think it is [2024] • asana.* Asana. https://asana.com/resources/inbox-zero

Weinschenk, S. (2012, September 18). The true cost of multi-tasking. Psychology Today. https://www.psychologytoday.com/us/blog/brain-wise/201209/the-true-cost-of-multi-tasking